IMPORTANT QUESTIONS OF ENVIRONMENTAL SCIENCE FOR NEET

GET READY FOR ENVIRONMENTAL KNOWLEDGE

K.BASU

To All Aspirants of NEET and other Exams.

Contents

1. Questions And Answers-i 1
2. Questions And Answers-ii 3
3. Questions And Answers -iii 5
4. Questions And Answers-iv 7
5. Questions And Answers-v 9
6. Questions And Answers-vi 11
7. Questions And Answers-vii (disease Series) 13
8. Questions And Answers-viii 15
9. Questions And Answers-ix 17
10. Questions And Answers-x 19

CHAPTER ONE

Questions and Answers-I

Q1. Which of the Following is not a site for "in-situ" method of Conservation of flora?

- a) Biosphere Reserve
- **b) Botanical Garden* (b is correct)**
- c) National Park
- d) Wildlife Sanctuary

- **Note:Difference between In-situ and Ex-situ method** : **"In-situ"** method, State government declared any forest area as **National park ,wild life sanctuary,Biosphere reserve** etc in order to **conserve flora and Fauna** .Where as,in case **"Ex-situ"** method , **Man-made environment** is developed to prorect or conserve flora and Fauna. Example like **Botanical garden, Zoos andAquarium etc.**

Q2. Which of following Institution published " RED DATA" Book related to flora and fauna conditions?

- a) UNEP
- **b) IUCN* (full form:** International Union for Conservation of Nature)
- c) UNFCCC
- d) IMO

Q3. Which of the following place recently UN climate change conference COP-26 meeting was held of year 2021?

- a) New York, US
- **b) Glasgow,Scotland***
- c) Paris,France
- d) Berlin,Germany

Q4. In which year the wild life protection Act was passed in India ?

- a) 1975
- **b)1972***
- c) 1973
- d)1974

Q5. "Project Tiger" was launched in India in which year ?

- a) 1975
- b)1972

- **c) 1973***
- d) 1974

Q6. First UN Earth Summit was held in which place and year?

- a) New York in 1994
- b)Berlin in 1992
- **c) Rio-de-janerio in Brazil in 1992***
- d) Paris in 1993

Q7. Presently, How many wetlands in India declared as "Ramsar" wetlands sites ?

- a) 50
- **b) 49***
- c) 45
- d) 42

Q8. Ramsar convention is related to which environmental issues in the world?

- a) Oceans
- b) deltas
- **c) wetlands***
- d) coastal

Q9. Which of the following protected area where local people are not allow to collect and use biomass?

- a) Biosphere
- **b) National park***
- c) Wetlands
- d) Wildlife sanctuary

Q10. Which of the following kinds of organisms act like a pollinating (pollen grains) agent/agents?

- a) Bee
- b) Bat
- c) Birds
- **d) All of the Above***

CHAPTER TWO

Questions and Answers-II

Q 1. Which of the following Layer of Atmosphere the "Ozone Layer" is situated on the earth?

- a) Troposphere
- **b) Stratosphere***
- c) Mesosphere
- d) Ionosphere

Q2 Which of the following Layer of Atmosphere below it the "life is exists" on the earth?

- **a) Troposphere***
- b) Stratosphere
- c) Mesosphere
- d) Ionosphere

Q3. Which of the following Layer show sudden increase in Temperature called "Temperature Inversion"?

- a) **Stratosphere***
- b) Mesosphere
- c) Troposphere
- d) Ionosphere

Q4. Which of the following rays radiates from Sun can cause Skin cancer ?

- a) Infrared rays
- **b) Ultraviolet rays***
- c) Microwaves
- d) Radiowaves

Q5. Which following rays radiates from Sun been stop by Ozone layer incoming to Earth surface?

- a) Infrared rays
- b) Microwaves
- **c) Ultraviolet rays***
- d) Radiowaves

Q6. Which of the following gas is responsible for depletion of Ozone layer?

- **a) Chlorofluorocarbons (CFCs)***

- b) Methane
- c) Carbon dioxide
- d) water vapour

Q7. which following unit is used to measure thickness of Ozone layer?

- a) Decibal
- **b) Dobson ***
- c) Dioptre
- d) Degree

Q8. Which of the following Protocol or convention related to "Ozone layer" depletion due to Green house gases?

- a) Kyoto Protocol
- **b) Montreal Protocol***
- c) Montreux Accord
- d) Paris Agreement

Q9. Which of the following is one of major source of green house effect?

- **a) Methane***
- b) Carbon dioxide
- c) Carbon monoxide
- d) Sulphur dioxide

Q10. Which of the following greenhouse gas responsible for increase of temperature of the Earth ?

- **a) Carbon dioxide***
- b) Carbon monoxide
- c) Sulphur dioxide
- d) Methane

CHAPTER THREE

Questions and Answers -III

Q1. Which one of the following national "Aquatic" Animal of India?

- a) Saltwater crocodile
- b) Olive ridley turtle
- **c) Gangetic Dolphin***
- d) Gharial

Q2. Which aquatic animal has larger size of brain than its body size?

- a) Blue Whale
- b) Killer Shark
- **c) Dolphin***
- d) Sperm Whale

Q3. Which of the following is most stable ecosystem on the earth?

- a) Desert
- **b) Oceans***
- c) River
- d) forest

Q4. Which of following ecosystem is largest ecosystem in environment?

- a) Terrestrial
- **b) Aquatic***
- c) Desert
- d) agriculture

Q5. Which of the following compounds responsible for Acid Rain?

- a) Carbon dioxide and carbon monoxide
- **b) Sulphur dioxide and nitrous oxide***
- c) methane and sulphur
- d) Sulphur oxide and Nitrogen oxide

Q6.Which of the following gas responsible for Bhopal gas tragedy in India ?

- **a) Methyl isocynate***

- b) Methyl isocynite
- c) Methyl nitrate
- d) Methyl cynide

Q7. Which of the following rays are released by the Earth?

- a) Ultraviolet
- **b) Infrared***
- c) Microwaves
- d) Radiowaves

Q8. Photochemical smog is a resultant of the reaction among of the following ?

- **a) NO_2,O_3 and peroxyacetyl nitrate in the presence of sunlight***
- b) CO_2,O_2 and peroxyacetyl nitrate in the presence of sunlight
- c) CO,CO_2 at low temperature
- d) High concentration of NO_2

Q9. In which year Animal welfare board was established in India ?

- a) 1961
- **b) 1962***
- c) 1963
- d) 1964

Q10. Who is head of National Ganga council in India?

- a) Home Minister
- **b) Prime Minister***
- c) Environment Minister
- d) Rural development minister

CHAPTER FOUR

Questions and Answers-IV

Q1. Which of the following is correct sequence of food chain in terrestrial ecosystem?

- a) Producers- Secondary consumers-Primary consumers-Tertiary consumers - Decomposers
- b) Secondary consumers-Primary consumers-Tertiary consumers-Producers-Decomposers
- **c)Producers- Primary consumers- Secondary consumers-Tertiary consumers-Decomposers***
- d) Secondary consumers-Primary consumers-Decomposers-Tertiary consumers-Producers

Q2. Who is head of National Board of Wildlife in India?

- **a) Prime Minister***
- b) Home Minister
- c) Environment Minister
- d) Urban development Minister

Q3. Prevention of cruelty to Animal act was passed in which year?

- a) 1962
- **b) 1960***
- c) 1963
- d) 1964

Q4. Which of the following region considered as a Rich Biodiversity Hotspot in India?

- a) Eastern Ghat
- **b) Western Ghat***
- c) Sunderbans
- d) chhotanagpur

Q5. Which of the following only riverine Island in India situated at Assam ?

- a) Ross Island
- **b) Majuli Island*(Brahmaputra river)**
- c) Money Island
- d) Wheeler Island

Q6. Which of the following "World first Floating National Park"situated near Loktak Lake in India ?

- **a) Keibul Lamjao National Park* (Manipur)**

- b) Namdampha National Park
- c) Dampa Tiger Reserve
- d) Kanha National Park

Q7. How much percentage of forest cover for efficient ecological environment ?

- a) 40%
- **b) 33%***
- c) 55%
- d) 45%

Q8. Biological Oxygen Demand (BOD) is an Aquatic ecosystem environmental issues results in?

- a) Increase of oxygen level
- **b) Decrease of oxygen level***
- c) Increase nitrogen dioxide
- d) Decrease nitrogen dioxide

Q9. The process by which an entire body of water enriched with minerals and nutrients?

- a) Sedimentation
- **b) Eutrophication***
- c) Evaporation
- d) Sublimation

Q10. H1N1 virus is also known as

- a) AIDS
- b) Bird Flu
- **c) Swine Flu***
- d) Dengue

CHAPTER FIVE

Questions and Answers-V

Q1. Which of the following Aquatic mammal was extinct from the Earth?

- a) Sea horse
- b) Sea cow
- c) Sea lion
- **d) dugong***

Q2. Which of the following process plants convert Light energy into chemical energy ?

- a) Photo chemical effect
- **b) Photosythesis***
- c) Photoeffect
- d) Sunlight effect

Q3. Which of the following chemical compound made by plants as food ?

- a) Sucrose
- **b) Glucose***
- c) Fructose
- d) All of the Above

Q4. Which following considered as renewable energy source?

- a) Nuclear energy
- b) thermal energy
- **c) solar energy***
- d) Biogas

Q5. Which of the following decomposer organism/organisms participate in the food chain in ecosystem?

- a) Virus
- **b) Fungi and Bacteria***
- c) Virus and Bacteria
- d) Fungi and Virus

Q6. Which of the following is known as Kharif crop or Summer crop?

- a) Wheat

- b) Pulses
- **c) Rice***
- d) Sugarcane

Q7. Which of the following is correct sequence of ecosystem in the order of decreasing productivity?

- a) Oceans,lake,grassland,mangroves
- b) mangroves,oceans,grassland,lakes
- **c) mangroves,grassland,lakes,oceans***
- d) oceans,mangroves,lakes,grassland

Q8. Which following is known as Rainforest?

- a) Tropical wet decidous forest
- **b) Tropical Evergreen Forest***
- c) Temperate Forest
- d) Tropical Dry Decidous Forest

Q9. Which of the following is indicator species which help to measure the level of Sulphur dioxide cause Air Pollution?

- a) Mosses
- **b) Lichens**
- c) Bacteria
- d) Moulds

Q10. Which of the following gas responsible for chronic poisoning in Humans?

- a) Carbon dioxide
- **b) Carbon monoxide***
- c) Carbide
- d) Nitrogen

CHAPTER SIX

Questions and Answers-VI

Q1. At which place the Headquater of International Solar Alliance is situated?

- a) New Delhi
- **b) Gurugram***
- c) Noida
- d) Meerut

Q2. At which direction energy flow in food chain of ecosystem?

- a) Bi directional
- **b) unidirectional**
- c) multidirectional
- d) bi lateral

Q3 Which following is correct sequence of ecological organisation?

- **a) Individual-Population-community-ecosystem-biome-biosphere***
- b) Population-community-ecosystem-Individual-biosphere
- c) biosphere-Population-community-ecosystem-Individual
- d) biosphere-Individual-Population-community

Q4. When pollutants enter in the food chain then this phenomena known as:

- a) Biomagnification
- **b) Bioaccumulation***
- c) Eutrophication
- d) sulphurization

Q5.When tendency of pollutant to increase concentration when it moves from one trophic level to another in food chain ?

- **a) Biomagnification***
- b) Eutrophication
- c) Bioaccumulation
- d) Sulphurization

Q6. Which following microorganism can decrease oxygen dissolved in water bodies due to Eutophication?

- a) Yeast
- b) Bacteria
- **c) Algal bloom***
- d) Virus

Q7. Which of following element can cause the Itai-Itai disease?

- a) Mercury
- **b) Cadmium***
- c) Magnesium
- d) Iron

Q8. Which following element can cause Minamata disease?

- **a) Mercury***
- b) Magnesium
- c) Cadmium
- d) Iron

Q9. Which of the following cause Blue-baby Syndrome in babies ?

- a) Nitrite
- **b) Nitrate***
- c) Nitrogen
- d) Nitrous Oxide

Q10. Which of the following is water borne disease due to contamination of water?

- a) sleeping sickness
- b) Plague
- **c) Diarrhea***
- d) Yellow fever

CHAPTER SEVEN

Questions and Answers-VII (Disease series)

Q1. Which of the follwing disease commonly known as Black Death?

- a) Corona
- b) Dengue
- **c) Plague***
- d) Malaria

Q2. Which of the following is disease that results nervous breakdown of brain in the children?

- **a) Japan Encephalitis***
- b) Kala Azar
- c) Sleeping Sickness
- d) Plague

Q3. Which of the following is main cause of Colour Blindness in Human?

- a) Due to deficiency of Vitamin A
- **b) Due to genetic disorder***
- c) Due to deficiency of Protein
- d) Due to deficiency of Hemoglobin

Q4. Which of the following type of mosquito that cause Dengue ?

- **a) Aedes aegypti***
- b) Anopheles
- c) culex
- d) parasitic

Q5. Which following body part is affected by Parkinson disease ?

- **a) Brain***
- b) Lungs
- c) Heart
- d) Stomach

Q6. Which of the following body part affected by Glaucoma disease and Pink eye disease means conjunctivitis?

- **a) Eyes***
- b) Ears
- c) Nose
- d) Mouth

Q7. Which of the following disease commonly known as Hansen disease?

- **a) Leprosy***
- b) Cataract
- c) Asthma
- d) Nervous breakdown

Q8. Full form of ECG:

- **a) Electrocardiogram*(Heart)**
- b) Electrocomputergram
- c) Electrocastogram
- d) Electrocomputegram

Q9. Full form of EEG:

- **a) Electroencephalogram (Brain)***
- b) Electroexitphalogram
- c) Electroexistphalogram
- d) Elytroencephlogram

Q10. Full form of BCG:

- **a) Bacillus Calmette-Guerin (TB)**
- b) Bacillus Calamite Guerin
- c) Bacillus Calanite Guerin
- d) Bacilous Calanine Guerin

CHAPTER EIGHT

Questions and Answers-VIII

Q1. Which of the following year Air (Prevention and Control of pollution Act) was passed in India?

- a) 1980
- **b)1981***
- c) 1985
- d) 1989

Q2.Which of the following year Water (Prevention and Control of pollution Act) was passed in India?

- a) 1975
- b) 1980
- **c)1974***
- d) 1969

Q3. In which year Bhopal gas tragedy was occured in India?

- a) 1986
- **b) 1984***
- c) 1985
- d) 1987

Q4. Who was/were the personalities play prominent role in chipko movement in India?

- a) Gaura Devi and Megha Patkar
- **b) Sunderlal Bahuguna and Gaura devi***
- c) Medha Patkar and Sunderlal Bahuguna
- d) Medha Patkar and Gaura Devi

Q5. Which of the following leader started Bhoodan Movement?

- a) Medha Patkar
- **b) Vinoba Bhave***
- c) Baba Amte
- d) Gaura Devi

Q6. Which of the following environmental Activist associated with Narmada Bachao Andolan?

- a) Megha Patkar

- **b) Medha Patkar***
- c) Mahima Patkar
- d) Mahima Padkar

Q7. On which river Sardar sarovar dam is constructed?

- a) Ganga
- b) Mahanadi
- **c) Narmada***
- d) Sutlej

Q8. Which of the following trophic level in food chain known as " Autotrophs"?

- **a) Producers***
- b) Primary consumers
- c) Secondary consumers
- d) Tertiary consumers

Q9. Which of the following trophic level in food chain known as "Saprotrophs"?

- **a) Detritus***
- b) Decomposers
- c) Primary consumers
- d) Tertiary consumers

Q10. Human beings are which type consumers:

- a) Herbivores
- **b) Omnivores***
- c) Carnivores
- d) Saprophytes

CHAPTER NINE

Questions and Answers-IX

Q1. Which of the following used as Artificial Sweetening Agent?

- a) Sucrose
- b) Maltose
- **c) Aspartame***
- d) Fructose

Q2. Which of following Drug is considered as main cause behind extinction of Vultures around the world ?

- **a) Diclofenac***
- b) Paracetamol
- c) Ramdesivir
- d) All of Above

Q3. Which following sugar considered as Sweetest sugar ?

- a) Maltose
- b) Sucrose
- **c) Fructose***
- d) Aspartame

Q4. Full form of DDT:

- a) Dichloro diphenyl tetrachloro ethane
- **b) Dichloro diphenyl trichloro ethane***
- c) Dichloro dimethyl trichloro ethane
- d) Dichloro diethyl tetrachloro ethane

Q5. Which following gas is not part of greenhouse gases?

- a) Methane
- **b) Hydrogen***
- c) sulphur dioxide
- d) carbon dioxide

Q6. Which of the following is largest source of methane gas on the Earth?

- a) Wheat

- **b) Paddy* or Rice***
- c) Maize
- d) Sugarcane

Q7. Which of the following is lightest gas in the world?

- **a) Hydrogen***
- b) Helium
- c) Nitrogen
- d) Oxygen

Q8. Which of the following is Heaviest Gas in the World?

- a) Argon
- b) Helium
- **c) Radon***
- d) Xenon

Q9.The most abundant metal in the earth's crust is:

- **a) Aluminium**
- b) oxygen
- c) silver
- d) gold

Q10. The most Abundant element on the earth's crust is:

- **a) Oxygen***
- b) Silica
- c) Aluminium
- d) Iron

CHAPTER TEN

Questions and Answers-X

Q1. Which of the following is a Biotic component?

- a) Water
- **b) Plants***
- c) Air
- d) Land

Q2. Which of the following is a Abiotic Component?

- a) Plants
- **b) Water***
- c) Animals
- d) Birds

Q3. Which of the following Mammals lays eggs ?

- a) Whale
- **b) Echidna***
- c) Bat
- d) All of Above

Q4. Which are following only Mammals can flight ?

- a) Platypus
- **b) Bat***
- c) Ostrich
- d) Kiwi

Q5. Which of the following correct sequence of Classification of Living organisms in taxonomy?

- a) kingdom, phylum, class, order,species,family and genus.
- **b) kingdom, phylum, class, order,family, genus, and species**
- c) family, genus, species,kingdom, phylum, class and order
- d) phylum, class ,order,family, genus, species and kingdom

9 798888 152546

Printed by Libri Plureos GmbH in Hamburg,
Germany